The PARTY MAGICIAN kit

Illustrated by John Headford
Text devised by Gordon Hill

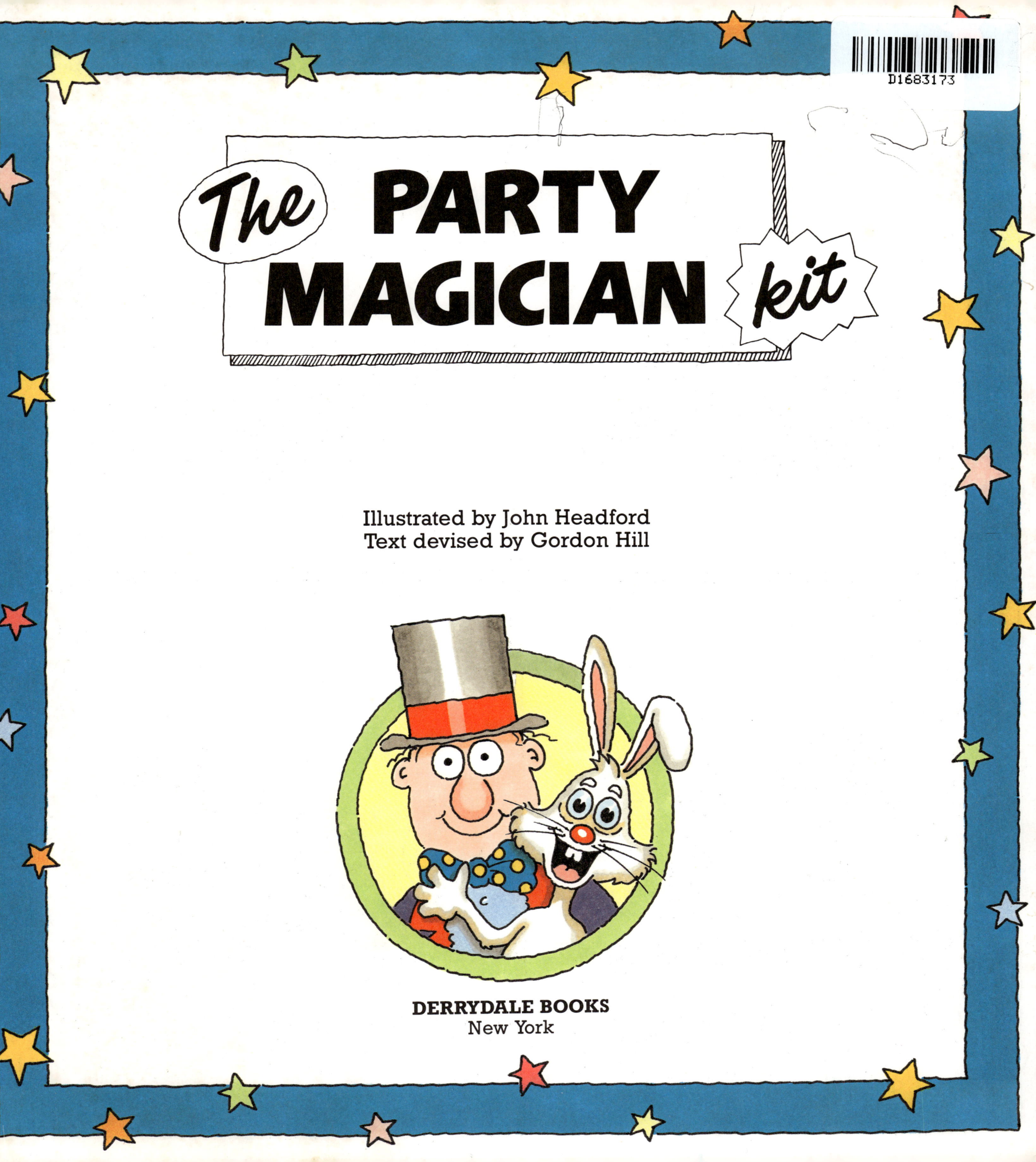

DERRYDALE BOOKS
New York

This is Your Card

All professional magicians have at least one card trick in their act. Here's an easy one to practice and try out on your audience.

1. Shuffle the cards and spread them out, faceup. Secretly look at and remember the card at the BOTTOM of the deck.

2. Turn the cards back facedown and ask your friend to take out any card.

3. Ask your friend to remember the card before placing it on top of the deck.

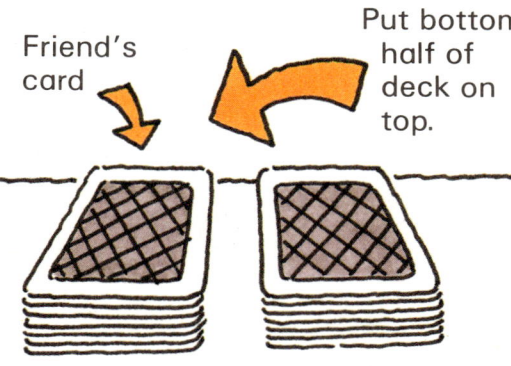

4. Cut the deck in two, and place the bottom half on top of the top half. The chosen card is now lost in the deck.

5. Spread the cards out faceup, as you look for your own card.

6. Your friend's card will be immediately to the RIGHT of the card you remembered. Take your friend's card from the deck.

7. Ask her which card she chose. Show her the card you are holding.

Dotty Diamonds

Fold your magic press-out playing card in half and glue the two halves together, as shown below. Now you're ready to amaze your friends!

Card has two diamonds on one side . . .

. . . and five on the other.

1. Show the side with two diamonds on it. Cover up the bottom diamond with your thumb. The card will look like an Ace.

2. Turn the card to the other side, but put your thumb over the diamond in the middle so the card looks like a four.

3. Turn the card over again. This time put your thumb over the blank space. Let the audience think it is a three, with your hand hiding a diamond.

4. Turn the card over and cover the blank space in the center, so it looks like a six.

5. If you want to, repeat the sequence again, so the card keeps on changing.

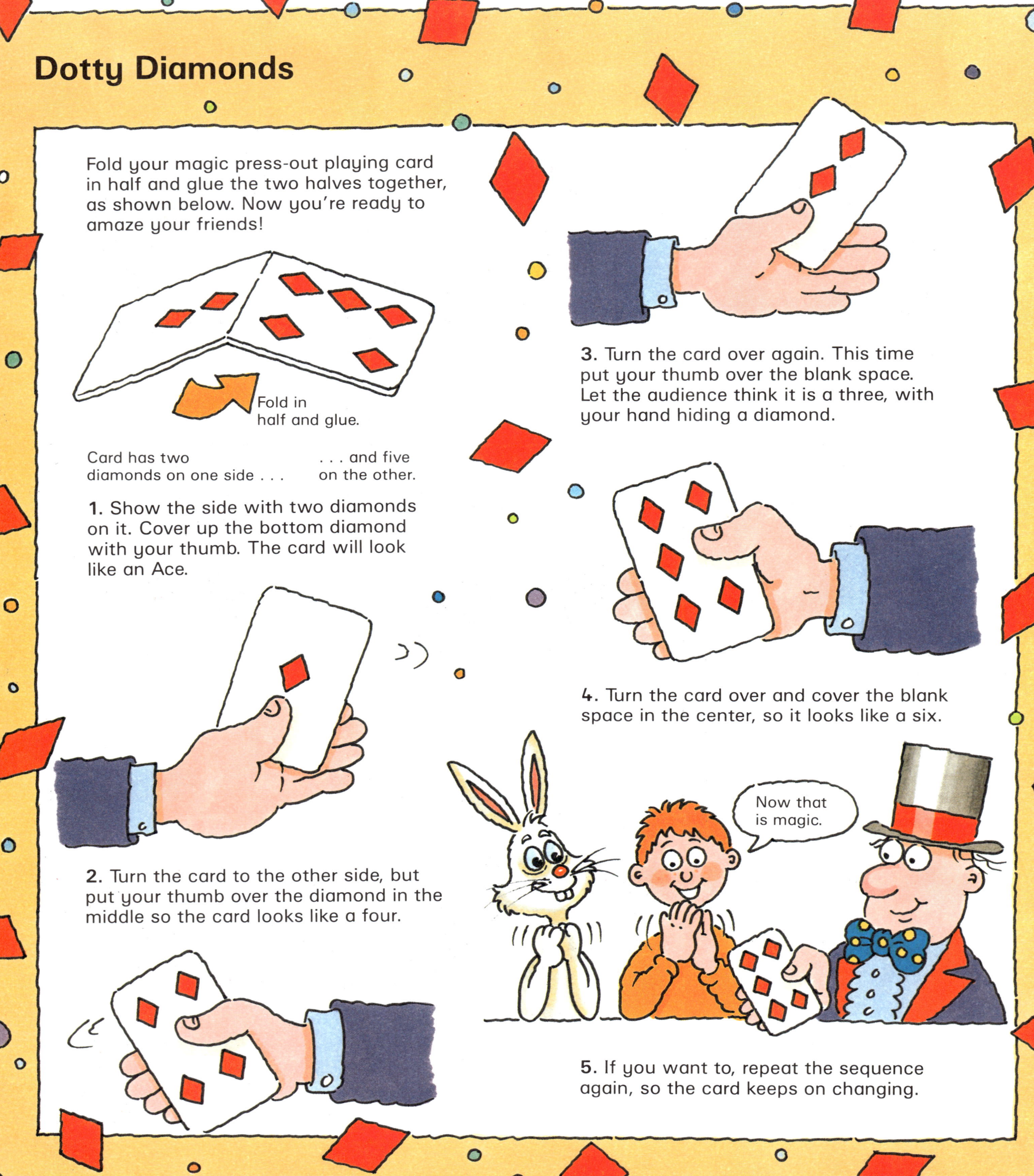

The Great Divide

Shock and then amaze your friends by sawing your assistant in two before their very eyes. All you need is a pair of scissors, an envelope, and the press-out assistant from the middle of this book.

1. Before you show the trick to your audience, seal the envelope and cut off each end, so you end up with a long tube.

2. Make two slits in one side of the envelope, as shown. Show your audience the assistant and the envelope, but NOT the secret slits.

3. Put the assistant into the envelope, secretly pushing her out through one slit and back into the envelope through the other slit.

4. Show the audience the press-out assistant in the tube. Don't let them see the other side, where the assistant is really outside the tube.

5. Now cut through the envelope, making sure that the scissors go between the assistant and the envelope tube, as shown.

6. The envelope can now be shown to your audience in two pieces. But your assistant is unharmed, just like the real trick!

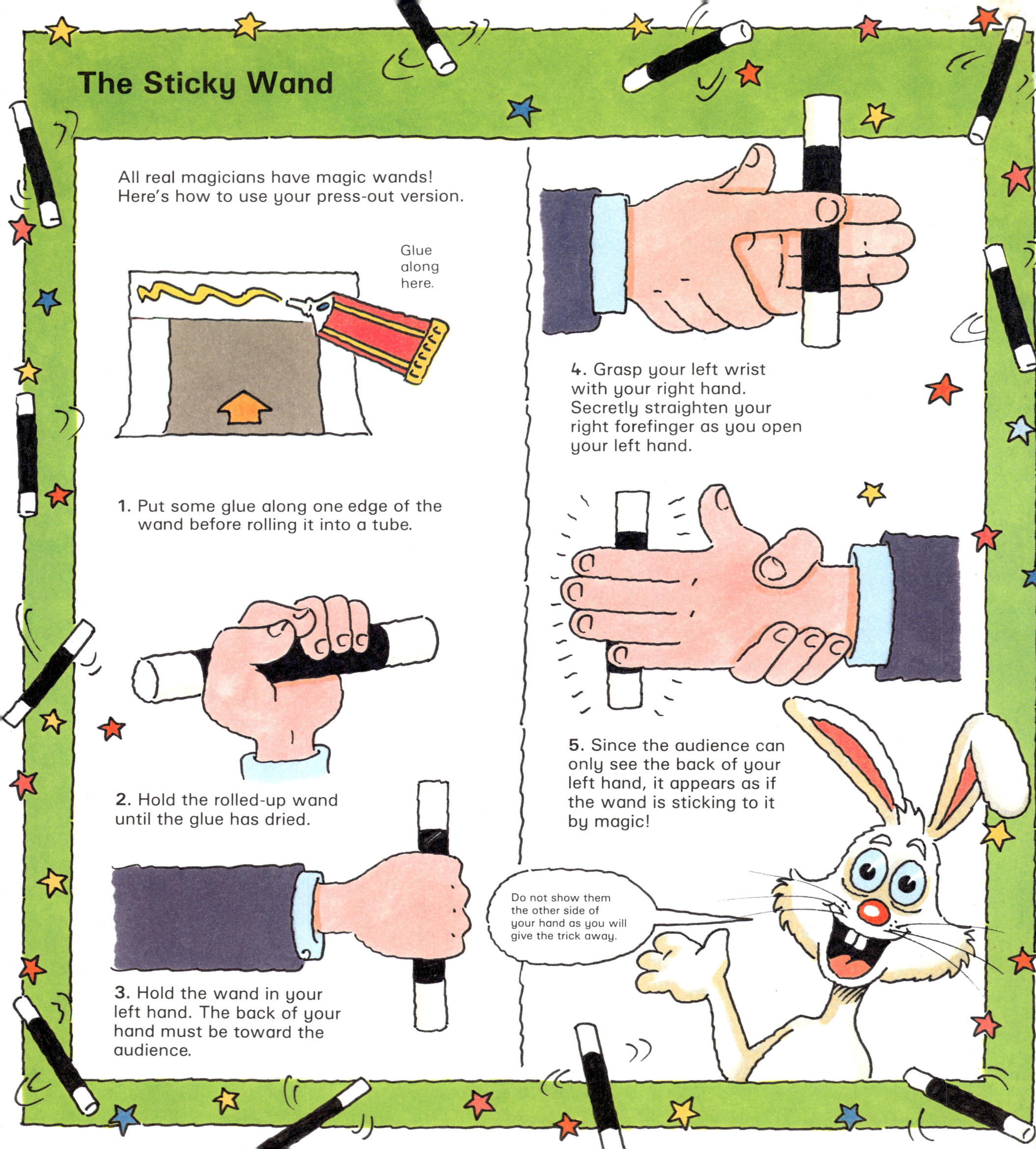

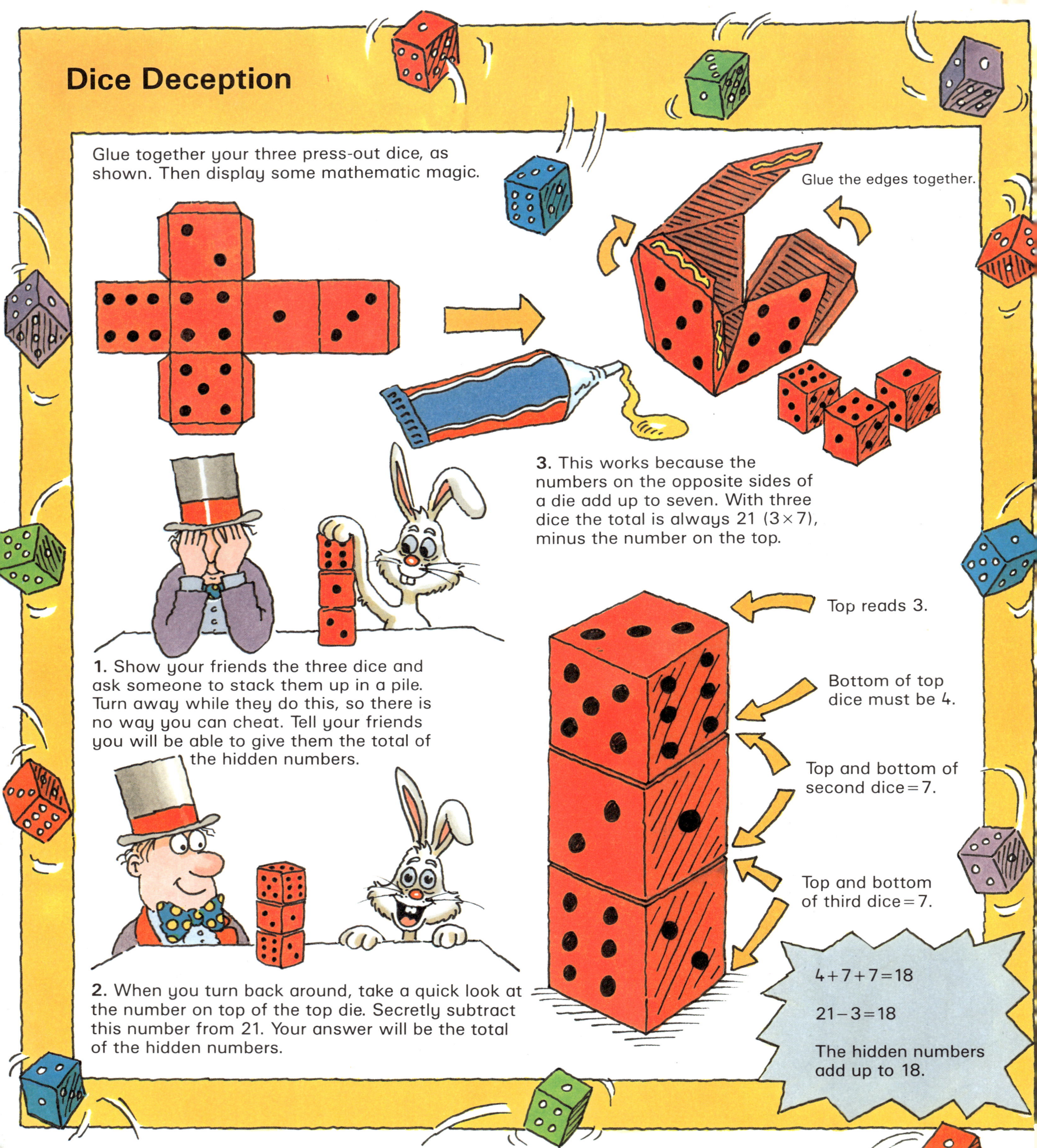

The Magic Boomerangs

Your fans are bound to come back if you show them your press-out boomerang routine. Press out the red and the blue boomerangs supplied.

1. Hold the blue one above the red one, as shown in the picture. The red one looks longer than the blue one.

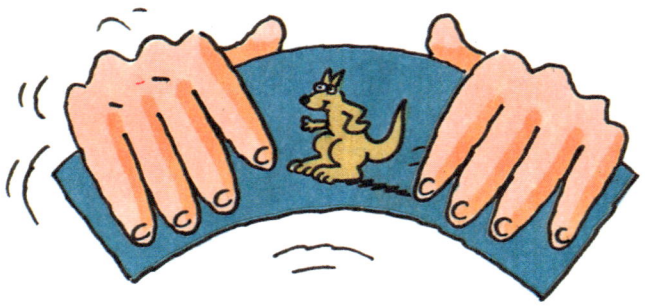

2. Pretend to stretch the blue boomerang.

3. Now hold the red one above the blue one. It now looks as though the blue one is the longer of the two!

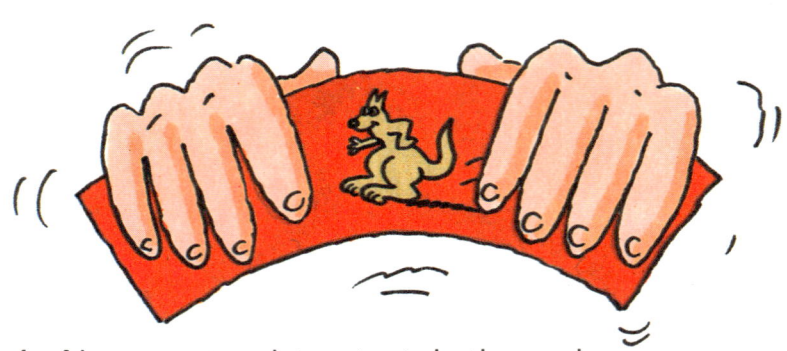

4. Now pretend to stretch the red boomerang and then hold the blue one above the red one.

5. The red one seems to be longer again!

6. To finish the trick, pretend to squeeze the red boomerang to make it smaller. Then hold the two boomerangs exactly on top of one another.

Tricky Tearing

For this terrific tearing trick, you need two strips of paper, each measuring about 8 inches long by 1 inch wide.

Fold one strip up, like this.

1. Fold one strip into a small bundle. Glue the bundle to one end of the second strip of paper.

Folded strip glued to one end of straight strip.

2. When the glue has dried, the trick is ready. Practice in front of a mirror before you show it to anyone.

3. Hold the strip of paper so that the bundle is hidden in one of your hands.

4. Tear the unfolded strip into small pieces. Collect the pieces in your other hand.

5. Now unfold the bundle, but keep the torn pieces hidden in your hand.